MicroWriter

William H. Starbuck

Produced by:
Brian Wiser & Bill Martens

 Apple PugetSound Program Library Exchange

MicroWriter

ACKNOWLEDGEMENTS

MicroWriter was programmed by William H. Starbuck of the University of Oregon in 1980, and this new book is being released with his permission.

MicroWriter was tested by A.P.P.L.E. staff member Steve Johnson.

PRODUCTION

Brian Wiser → Design, Layout, Editing
Bill Martens→ Editing, Proofreading

DISCLAIMER

About the Author

William H. Starbuck

William Starbuck is courtesy professor-in-residence at the Lundquist College of Business of the University of Oregon and professor emeritus at New York University. He received his M.S. and Ph.D. in industrial administration at Carnegie Institute of Technology, after receiving an A.B. in physics at Harvard. He also received a Ph.D. honoris causa in social science from Stockholm University and the title Docteur honoris causa from both the Université Panthéon-Assas (Paris II) and the Université Paul Cézanne (Aix-Marseille III).

He has held faculty positions at Purdue University, the Johns Hopkins University, Cornell University, the University of Wisconsin-Milwaukee, and New York University, as well as visiting positions at ESSEC Business School, London Graduate School of Business Studies, Norwegian School of Economics and Business Administration, the University of Gothenburg, Stockholm School of Economics, Université de Versailles Saint-Quentin-en-Yvelines, the University of Canterbury, Université de Paris IX - Dauphine, the University of Oregon, University of Aix-Marseille III, Université de Paris I – La Sorbonne, and the University of South Florida, and the University of Oxford. He was also a senior research fellow at the International Institute of Management, Berlin.

He has been the editor of *Administrative Science Quarterly*, chaired the screening committee for senior Fulbright awards in business management, directed the doctoral program in business administration at New York University, and he was the President of the Academy of Management. He is a member of the Council of the Society for the Advancement of Management Studies.

He formerly served on the editorial boards of the Academy of Management Review, Accounting, Management and Information Technologies, Administrative Science Quarterly, the British Journal of

Management, the Journal of Applied Social Psychology, the Journal of Leadership Studies, the Journal of Management Inquiry, the Journal of Socioeconomics, Knowledge Management and Information Studies, and Organization.

He currently serves on the editorial boards of the Asian Case Research Journa, Information and Organization, the International Journal of Management Reviews, the Journal of Management Studies, Organization Management Journal, and the Scandinavian Journal of Management. He is a fellow of the Academy of Management, the American Psychological Association, the Association for Psychological Science, the British Academy of Management, and the Society for Industrial and Organizational Psychology, and a member of Sigma Xi.

He has published over 160 articles on accounting, bargaining, business strategy, computer programming, computer simulation, forecasting, decision making, human-computer interaction, learning, organizational design, organizational growth and development, perception, scientific methods, and social revolutions. He has also written two books and edited 17 books, including the two-volume *Handbook of Organizational Design*, which was chosen the best book on management published during 1982. His 2006 book, *The Production of Knowledge*, reflects on lessons from his own academic journey and on the challenges associated with management and social science research.

About the Producers

Brian Wiser

Brian Wiser is a long-time consultant, enthusiast and historian of Apple, the Apple II and Macintosh. Steve Wozniak and Steve Jobs, as well as *Creative Computing*, *Nibble*, *InCider*, and *A+* magazines were early influences.

Brian designed, edited, and co-produced many books including: *Nibble Viewpoints: Business Insights From The Computing Revolution*, *Cyber Jack: The Adventures of Robert Clardy and Synergistic Software*, *Synergistic Software: The Early Games*, *The Colossal Computer Cartoon Book: Enhanced Edition*, *What's Where in the Apple: Enhanced Edition*, and *The WOZPAK: Special Edition* – an important Apple II historical book with Steve Wozniak's restored original, technical handwritten notes.

He passionately preserves and archives all facets of Apple's history, and noteworthy related companies such as Beagle Bros and Applied Engineering, featured on AppleArchives.com. His writing, interviews and books are featured on the technology news site CallApple.org and in *Call-A.P.P.L.E.* magazine that he co-produces. Brian also co-produced the retro iOS game *Structris*.

In 2005, Brian was cast as an extra in Joss Whedon's movie *Serenity*, leading him to being a producer and director for the documentary film *Done The Impossible: The Fans' Tale of Firefly & Serenity*. He brought some of the *Firefly* cast aboard his Browncoat Cruise and recruited several of the *Firefly* cast to appear in a film for charity. Brian speaks about his adventures to large audiences at conventions around the country.

Bill Martens

Bill Martens is a systems engineer specializing in office infrastructures and has been programming since 1976. The DEC PDP 11/40 with ASR-33 Teletypes and CRT's were his first computing platforms with his first forays in the Apple world coming with the Apple II computer.

Influences in Bill's computing life came from *Byte* magazine, *Creative Computing* magazine, and *Call-A.P.P.L.E.* magazine as well as his mentors Samuel Perkins, Don Williams, Joff Morgan, and Mike Christensen.

Bill is a co-producer of many books including *What's Where in the Apple: Enhanced Edition, The WOZPAK: Special Edition, Nibble Viewpoints: Business Insights From The Computing Revolution,* and co-programmer for the iOS version of the retro game *Structris*. He has written many articles which have appeared in user group newsletters and magazines such as *Call-A.P.P.L.E.*.

Bill worked for Apple Pugetsound Program Library Exchange (A.P.P.L.E.) under Val Golding and Dick Hubert as a data manager and programmer in the 1980s, and is the current president of the A.P.P.L.E. user group established in 1978. He reorganized A.P.P.L.E. and restarted *Call-A.P.P.L.E.* magazine in 2002. He is the production editor for the A.P.P.L.E. website CallApple.org, writes science fiction novels in his spare time, and is a retired semi-pro football player.

CONTENTS

Welcome to *MicroWriter*

A disk image of the *MicroWriter* software can be downloaded from the publisher's site: www.callapple.org. The first thing to learn is how to move the cursor. The cursor is that flashing square in the top left corner of the screen. It shows you where your actions will take effect. For instance, characters you type emerge beside the cursor, and the characters you delete are the ones just left of the cursor.

To move the cursor down, press the down-arrow key, located in the bottom-right corner of the keyboard. Try that now. If you want to move the cursor down several lines, you can hold the arrow key down.

When you move the cursor into the bottom four lines of the screen, the display shifts, bringing additional text into view. You should do that when you have read to the bottom of the screen.

All four arrow keys move the cursor. Try them out – left, right, down, and up. The left and right arrows shift the cursor one character at a time. The up and down arrows shift the cursor approximately one line at a time: 38 characters with a 40-column display, and 78 characters with an 80-column display.

When you are creating or revising text, or just reading it as you are now, you are editing. Pressing ESC lets you ESCape from editing: the cursor jumps to the editing menu that you saw when *MicroWriter* first became active. Do not panic if you press ESC by accident. No harm has been done. Just respond to the menu by pressing S for "See the text that is in memory".

This command makes the cursor jump right back to its previous position in this text. Indeed, why not test these actions out? Take note of the cursor's current position, ESCape to the menu, and then respond to the menu by pressing S (See). Does the cursor end up where it starts out?

Safety First

If you have not already done so, you should stop right here and make a backup copy (or two) of the *MicroWriter* disk. File the original *MicroWriter* disk in a safe spot, and use a copy. You can copy

MicroWriter with the program *COPYA* that comes with DOS 3.3. To use *COPYA* right now, insert the DOS 3.3 System Master in Drive 1, then depress three keys at the same time: the OPEN-APPLE (just left of the space bar), CONTROL, and lastly RESET.

The *MicroWriter* disk is full and you will add files on it while going through these instructions, so you should delete from the copies (not the original) a few files that you will not need. In particular, you only need Configuration Block.S if you set out to configure *MicroWriter* for a printer I have omitted. You also will not need the three-sector-long binary files that bear the names of printers you do not own. You can use *FID*, another program that comes with DOS 3.3, to UNLOCK and DELETE unneeded files.

Getting Control

An important principle is that depressing the CONTROL key changes most of the other keys into control keys. If you press only CONTROL and no other keys, nothing will happen: the computer does not even know that you pressed CONTROL. If you press H without depressing CONTROL, you will insert H's into this text at the cursor's location. But if you press H while you are holding down CONTROL, the computer takes an action. Your holding down CONTROL tells the computer to make no insertions and to interpret your other key presses as instructions.

Try CONTROL-H. First, depress the CONTROL key. Do not release it – hold it down. Now press the H key as well, just press it briefly. Then you can release the CONTROL key.

Surprise! CONTROL-H produces the same movements as the left arrow. Now try holding down CONTROL-H, that is, hold down H as well as CONTROL. This is equivalent to holding down the left arrow. Next, try CONTROL-U.

You have discovered a general principle: the four arrows and ESC, TAB, DELETE, and RETURN are merely well-labelled duplicates of various CONTROL codes.

2

CONTROL-L	CONTROL-I	CONTROL-[	CONTROL-M
DELETE	TAB	ESC	RETURN

CONTROL-H	CONTROL-J	CONTROL-K	CONTROL-U
<-	|	^	->
	V	|	

Because the arrows, ESC, TAB, DELETE, and RETURN are meaningful labels, you need not remember the equivalent CONTROL codes. I have explained these equivalences because they introduce the idea of a CONTROL code and because you may press these CONTROL codes by accident and then wonder why you got the results you did. Also, you may find CONTROL-L a useful substitute for DELETE.

But do not waste this opportunity to practice using the CONTROL key. Try the combinations of CONTROL with U, H, J, and K. Avoid CONTROL-I until you have read about TAB, and avoid CONTROL-L until you have read about DELETE.

Putting on Some Fast Moves

When you hold down the up arrow, the cursor moves upward quite briskly. But, even this speed is too slow for working with long documents, so *MicroWriter* offers you four faster movements. The rapid-movement keys cluster in the keyboard's bottom-left corner.

CONTROL-A	Up to the document's beginning.
CONTROL-S	Up many – about 12 lines.
CONTROL-Z	Down to the document's end.
CONTROL-X	Down many – about 12 lines.

For example, CONTROL-A shifts the cursor all the way to the beginning of the document, where you first saw it. After you press CONTROL-A, there is a short pause while the computer makes adjustments, then in a magical flash, the screen shows the start of these instructions.

You can remember these keys mainly by their positions and partly by their letters. The fast-movement keys occupy the bottom-left corner of the keyboard. A, the beginning of the alphabet, symbolizes the document's beginning. Z, the end of the alphabet, symbolizes the document's end. The two keys that cause 12-line movements are next to the A and Z. Also, the two keys that cause upward movements (A and S) sit above the two keys that produce downward movements (Z and X). You should find CONTROL-S and CONTROL-X helpful for moving through these instructions.

Why *MicroWriter* Works As It Does

MicroWriter aims to be a semi-professional word processor. It is more complex than the simplest word processors, and simpler than the most complex ones. I intend it for people who write often and who think about what they are typing while they are typing it.

MicroWriter's properties derive from my own experiences as a user. My ideas about word processing were shaped initially by a processor called *Apple Writer* that Paul Lutus wrote and Apple Computer sold. Better than its successor *Apple Writer][*, the first *Apple Writer* exhibited a lovely simplicity. But it also had some quirks and frustrating limitations. I tried alternatives such as *Wordstar, Screen Writer II*, and *Bank Street Writer.* My dissatisfaction led me to start creating word processors of my own design, which I tested in my daily work. Dozens of successors gradually evolved into *MicroWriter.* Then the reactions of two users, Del Clear and Steve Johnson, led to more improvements.

Some word processors remind their users constantly of the actions available – these processors are easier to learn than *MicroWriter.* And for people who use a word processor infrequently, these have the advantage of minimizing the demands on users' memories. However, the screen space devoted to reminding users about control actions cuts down on the screen space available for users' writings. *MicroWriter* shows as much text as possible so that you can see your words in context. If you write regularly, you will soon memorize *MicroWriter's* codes, whereas a word processor designed for quick learning and infrequent use would likely impede your writing.

4

MicroWriter does offer you two kinds of reminders. After you initiate a complex action such as Find or Transfer, *MicroWriter* reminds you what to do. Also, you can View a series of six help displays whenever you want: either press V in response to the editing menu or press CONTROL-V while you are editing. Why not press CONTROL-V now and look at these help displays, even though most of the control actions have yet to be explained? To change from one display to the next, press any key. After the sixth display, you will end up back here, with the cursor in its present position.

More complex than *MicroWriter* are word processors that always show text as it would print on paper, and offer fancy options such as two-column formats, fully justified text, or mass-production of form letters. These are appropriate for professional typists or printing firms, but my friends and I have found them less useful for writers who reflect while typing. The constant rearranging distracts you, you can easily get caught up in how your text looks rather than what it says, and the small 80-column letters are hard to read. More importantly, numerous options require numerous control codes that put the computer into different "modes." Both multiple modes and multitude control codes have detrimental effects: they raise error rates, make it more difficult to learn to use a word processor, slow down writing, and make it harder to remember how to do things.

MicroWriter has very few modes (even a typewriter has the modes shift and shiftlock). While you are editing, you can initiate any control action at nearly any time. The exceptions are obvious. For instance, you cannot start a new control action while the computer is still performing another action. *MicroWriter* ignores keys you press too early.

MicroWriter also has only 26 control actions, and you can initiate every control action in the same way: hold down CONTROL and press an alphabetic key. However, as you have already seen, it is better to use the arrows and ESC, TAB, DELETE, and RETURN to generate those CONTROL codes.

MicroWriter knows most of the rules and codes necessary to use your printer effectively, and it helps you exploit your printer's capabilities. You can change printing very flexibly without having to remember numerical codes.

If your computer contains an Apple 80-column text card, *MicroWriter* will automatically shift to an 80-column display when previewing how text would look on paper. You can also choose whether you want to see 40 columns or 80 columns while you are editing, and you can alter the number of columns displayed at any time. To change from a 40-column to an 80-column display, or vice versa:

1. ESCape to the menu

2. Respond to the menu by pressing A for "Alter the columns displayed."

3. Press S (See).

MicroWriter arrives with a 40-column display because I prefer it for editing. One reason is that the cursor responds more than twice as fast with a 40-column display, since the screen contains half as many characters and *MicroWriter* does less work to display each character. With an 80-column display, the cursor moves sluggishly. I also prefer a 40-column display because the large characters have better shapes, they can be seen well with the screen at lower brightness, and looking at a multitude of small characters for long periods makes me tired.

Editing Versus Printing

Writing with *MicroWriter* involves two steps. First, you create text with *MicroWriter* in editing mode. You type each paragraph of text as a continuous unit, pressing RETURN only at the end of the paragraph. You do not have to indent the first line of a paragraph, though you can do so. *MicroWriter* breaks the text into lines that fit the screen, but these lines do not correspond to the lines that would be printed on paper.

Second, you print the text, after specifying margins, paragraph indentations, and spacing between lines. In printing mode, *MicroWriter* breaks the text into lines of the right lengths to fit the margins. If you want to see your text as it would be printed before you actually commit it to paper, you can preview it.

Besides margins, editing and printing differ mainly in the reactions to printing codes, which are signals you can use to tell *MicroWriter* how to print. In editing mode, *MicroWriter* displays any printing codes you insert into text, but the codes do not affect the way your text looks. In printing mode, the printing codes themselves become invisible, but you can see their effects.

ESCape to the menu. Remember that S (See) will bring you back here. Notice that the menu's heading says it gives you options for "editing", and observe that one of these options is "Q = Quit to printing". *MicroWriter* actually has two menus – one for editing and the other for printing. If you respond to the editing menu by pressing Q (Quit), you will see the printing menu, which offers you the complementary option "Q = Quit to editing".

In fact, you can Quit directly from here to the printing menu by pressing CONTROL-Q, although you will have to return to here via the editing menu. Try it. Press CONTROL-Q and Quit to the printing menu, then respond to the printing menu by pressing Q (Quit), and lastly respond to the editing menu by pressing S (See). You will end up right back here, and the cursor will not have moved.

All of *MicroWriter's* facilities are available to you all of the time: they appear on two menus solely because a single long menu would be very hard to read.

When responding to a menu, you can hold down CONTROL or not, as you please. For instance, you can initiate reading by pressing R or CONTROL-R: pressing R is simpler, but pressing CONTROL-R maintains consistency with what you do while editing. *MicroWriter* can equate both types of commands because it knows you are not entering text when you are looking at a menu.

Starting to Edit

When you begin using *MicroWriter* and you first see the editing menu, you should do one of two things. Either press C for "Clear the memory and start a new file," or press R for "Read a file from disk." If you press C (Clear), you will see a blank screen with the cursor in the top-left corner. If you press R (Read), you will also see a screen with the cursor in the top-left corner, but the screen will show the file that you had *MicroWriter* read. (Any unit of text recorded on disk is called a file. A file might be a long document or just a few words.)

Both C (Clear) and R (Read) erase any text that was in the memory. If you want to preserve the text that is already in the memory, you should press S (See) instead. Any of these actions (C, S, and R) puts *MicroWriter* into editing mode.

Creating Text

You can type as if the Apple were a typewriter – pressing keys produces characters at the location of the cursor. The SHIFT key changes lower-case letters to upper-case, and changes numbers to special characters. Try typing now. First, move the cursor to whatever location suits you, say the end of a paragraph, then type some sentences, words, or numbers. Do not worry about harming these instructions – the unaltered version of the instructions is intact on the *MicroWriter* disk. Notice that your typing is inserted between the characters that are already here, it does not replace them. If you move the cursor to the middle of a word and then type, the new characters are inserted into the middle of the word.

You should mark the end of each paragraph by pressing RETURN. Although you cannot see it, this puts an invisible carriage-return symbol into your text. You do not have to indent the first line of a new paragraph, because *MicroWriter* assumes that the next character after a carriage return starts a new paragraph.

The combinations down-arrow-up-arrow and up-arrow-down-arrow are so useful that you should regard them as additional control codes. Suppose that while entering text, you notice an error you made several characters ago. You move the cursor back to the error by holding down the left arrow, and make the correction. Now you want to return to the end of the paragraph, where you were entering text. You could go back by holding down the right arrow. It is quicker, however, to press the down arrow and then the up arrow. The cursor jumps down one line and then up one line, but it does not end up just where it started out – it ends up at the end of the paragraph.

When performed on a line that ends with a carriage return, down-arrow-up-arrow moves the cursor to the position just before the carriage return. Complementarily, when performed on a line that follows a carriage return, up-arrow-down-arrow moves the cursor to the beginning of the line, which is usually the start of a paragraph.

The Apple's CAPS LOCK differs from the shiftlock on a typewriter. A typewriter's shiftlock would change the numbers into special symbols, you would turn off the shiftlock by pressing SHIFT, and consequently you could not use the SHIFT while the shiftlock is on. The Apple's CAPS LOCK does not affect the numbers or punctuation marks, you turn off the CAPS LOCK by pressing the CAPS LOCK itself, and you superimpose the SHIFT on the CAPS LOCK in order to get special characters instead of numbers.

MicroWriter's TAB also differs from that on a typewriter. The TAB key (or CONTROL-I) inserts several blanks into your text, so you can TAB to indent the first lines of paragraphs or to space between the columns of numerical tables. Press TAB now: *MicroWriter* will insert 5 spaces at the cursor's location. The TABbing number is 5 when *MicroWriter* begins so that you can TAB 5 spaces at the start of each paragraph.

If you want to change the TABbing number, press CONTROL-N for Number. *MicroWriter* will ask you how many spaces you want to TAB. Type a numerical answer, followed by RETURN to tell the computer that you have finished typing. Your answer will remain the TABbing number until you change it again.

You have just run across another general principle – press RETURN to tell *MicroWriter* that you are done providing information. You only have to do this when the input might require more than one character – if *MicroWriter* can react without your pressing RETURN, it will do so. *MicroWriter* waits for you to press RETURN after typing a TABbing number because you might enter more than one digit.

In these instructions and in *MicroWriter's* prompting messages, the term "enter" signals that you may have to press RETURN after providing information.

Deleting Text

You know how to generate text, including the insertion of new characters into existing text. But how do you get rid of characters you don't want?

MicroWriter offers you three levels of deletion: you can delete one character at a time, one word at a time, or one paragraph. First put the cursor immediately to the right of the characters you want to delete. Then:

`CTRL-L or DELETE`	Delete one character
`CTRL-O or CTRL-]`	Delete one word and the space to its left
`CTRL-P or CTRL-\`	Delete one paragraph

Note that all six keys (O, P, L,], \ and DELETE) sit close together at the upper right end of the keyboard. Each instruction has two CONTROL codes because some users may find it easier to remember letters and other users may prefer to recall positions. O, P, and L form one cluster: you can think of O as indicating word Out, P as symbolizing Paragraph out, and L as symbolizing Letter out. DELETE,], and \ form another cluster:] and \ sit just below DELETE, but you will have to remember that word deletion is on the left and paragraph deletion on the right.

During a deletion, the cursor moves from right to left. This may seem weird, but it serves a purpose. *MicroWriter* saves the deleted characters in a wastebasket so that you can recover them if you want. By storing the deleted characters in right-to-left sequence, *MicroWriter* can recover the characters in left-to-right sequence, as if you were typing them. You can recover characters at two rates:

`CONTROL-G`	Recover one character
`CONTROL-Y`	Recover 256 characters

Observe that Y shares the top row of alphabetic keys with the paragraph-deletion keys (P and \). G to recover one letter shares the middle row with L to delete one letter. You may be able to remember G by thinking of Getting a deleted letter back, and Y by thinking of Yanking many characters out of the wastebasket.

The wastebasket holds 1024 characters, and it operates as an endless ring. When you delete one character or one word at a time, the newly deleted characters are added to the wastebasket until it holds 1024 characters, and thereafter, the newly deleted characters replace the oldest characters in the wastebasket. Thus, you can never recover more than 1024 characters. This is a lot, but some paragraphs do exceed 1024 characters. So that you can always recover what you just deleted, *MicroWriter* limits paragraph deletions to 1024 characters. When you press CONTROL-P or CONTROL-\, *MicroWriter* deletes an entire paragraph only if that paragraph contains 1024 characters or less. If the paragraph is longer, *MicroWriter* stops deleting after 1024 characters and reports this to you.

This would be a good time to try the various deletion and recovery actions. You could go back to the place where you entered text and edit what you entered. As before, do not worry about messing up these instructions: the unaltered instructions remain on the *MicroWriter* disk. If your experiments make the instructions hard to read, or if you merely want to tidy up, ESCape to the editing menu and press R and Read the instructions into the computer again.

You can accelerate deletion and recovery by holding keys down. For instance, try holding DELETE down, then Get back what you deleted by holding down CONTROL-G.

Once again press CONTROL-V. The first two help displays should make much more sense to you now.

Moving Text

Deletion and recovery afford you simple ways to move short chunks of text around. For example, hold down CONTROL-O or CONTROL-] to delete a few words, move the cursor to another location, then hold down CONTROL-G to Get the deleted words back. To move a short paragraph, delete it with CONTROL-P or CONTROL-\, move the cursor to the desired location, then Yank the paragraph back with a CONTROL-Y or two. If CONTROL-Y recovers too much, delete the excess by holding down DELETE or CONTROL-L.

You can make moving text a bit easier by adding a carriage return. Put the cursor at the end of the passage you want to move. Before deleting, press RETURN. Then delete to the beginning of the passage – the added carriage return will go into the wastebasket just before the text does. Move the cursor to the desired location and yank the passage back. The extra carriage return will come out of the wastebasket just after the text that you want. Now you can delete any excess with CONTROL-P or CONTROL-\.

Of course, the delete-and-recover method will only move segments of 1024 characters or less. You can use CONTROL-T to Transfer text segments of any length. First, take note of the last characters of the segment you intend to transfer – you have to know enough characters to identify the segment's end uniquely. To minimize your typing, just insert an unusual symbol such as # or ~ at the end of the segment, then this single character is enough to identify where the segment ends. Second, move the cursor to the beginning of the segment, press CONTROL-T, and follow *MicroWriter's* prompting. Calling it Transfile, *MicroWriter* records the segment on the disk in whichever drive is active. Then when you press CONTROL-R, *MicroWriter* reads Transfile into the text at the cursor's location.

When you are moving text, you should not ESCape to the menu until you have finished. The menu display resets the wastebasket: this does not actually erase the deleted text, but you might have to recover the entire contents of the wastebasket in order to find the text you were moving. The menu display also terminates any incomplete Transfer: this is only a minor inconvenience, however, because you can complete the Transfer by using CONTROL-R to Read Transfile (as explained later).

As a learning experiment, you could use CONTROL-T to transfer this whole section to the beginning of these instructions.

More to Come

These instructions continue in a second file named Instructions 2. ESCape to the menu, then press R (Read). When *MicroWriter* asks if you want to read a file named Instructions, answer N for No. Type the file name Instructions 2 and press RETURN.

Reading and Writing Files on Disk

You can Write a text segment by pressing CONTROL-W. (Write is computer jargon for "record".) As with a Transfer, before you press CONTROL-W, you should either note the segment's last characters or insert an unusual character at the segment's end. After you press CONTROL-W, *MicroWriter* prompts your actions, recording the segment under a file name you choose. Because Apple DOS requires that every file name begin with a letter, *MicroWriter* rejects names that begin otherwise.

When you want to record an entire file from beginning to end, you can use CONTROL-W while you are in editing mode, but it is easier to ESCape to the editing menu and then to press W for "Write a file onto disk". You do not have to say how the file ends and you do not have to move the cursor to the file's beginning, because *MicroWriter* performs these actions and records the entire file. You may notice a brief delay just after you press W (Write) – *MicroWriter* is moving the cursor to the end of the file, and this delay is like the one after a CONTROL-Z.

It is a good practice to Write a backup copy of your text every so often as insurance against big mistakes or electrical outages. (Do not Write on the original *MicroWriter* disk a file with a locked name such as Instructions 2 because you might muck up the instructions permanently.)

When you respond R to the editing or printing menu, *MicroWriter* clears the memory before Reading. Any text in memory before you pressed R is lost. By contrast, CONTROL-R in editing mode lets you add a second file to the one in memory. First move the cursor to the location where you want the file inserted, then press CONTROL-R to Read the file. You can, for instance, Read here the last segment you transferred: press CONTROL-R and ask for Transfile.

CONTROL-R enables you to construct individualized letters or reports. For example, I do quite a bit of editing, and many authors overuse passive verbs, so I Read a standardized paragraph about passive verbs into editorial reports, then modify it to fit particular cases.

You can also create a glossary of long or complex phrases that you type often. For instance, you could Write the printing codes that you usually use to start a document, naming these codes New. File, then you could Read New.File instead of typing the codes anew. Similarly, you could record the printing codes for a heading under the name Heading, and the codes for ordinary text under the name Text. Or you could record the various indentations for writing in outline form under the names Out 0, Out 1, Out 2.

To switch back and forth between Drive 1 and Drive 2, you can press CONTROL-E while in editing mode or respond E, for "Exchange disk drives," to the editing menu. If Drive 1 is active, Exchange activates Drive 2, and if Drive 2 is active, Exchange activates Drive 1. You can also append ",D1" or ",D2" to file names.

To see what files a disk holds or to issue DOS commands such as RENAME, LOCK, or UNLOCK, either press CONTROL-D while you are editing, or press D to "catalog and issue Disk commands" in response to the editing menu. To get the basic idea, press CONTROL-D now, then just press RETURN instead of entering a DOS command. You will find out more about CONTROL-D later.

Try out these disk operations. First, press CONTROL-W and Write a text segment such as this paragraph. Give the segment a short file name such as Seg. Observe that *MicroWriter* does not delete the recorded segment from the text. Second, press CONTROL-D and verify that *MicroWriter* actually added Seg to the disk. Third, press CONTROL-R and Read the file at the cursor's location. If you did not move the cursor after Writing the file, the cursor will be sitting at the end of the segment you wrote, and after you Read it, the segment will appear twice in succession. Fourth, press CONTROL-D again and verify that the disk still holds Seg. Fifth, the editing menu enables you to delete a file by pressing DELETE. ESCape to the menu and press DELETE: when *MicroWriter* asks what file you want to delete, specify Seg. Sixth, press D in response to the menu and observe that Seg no longer exists. Lastly, to come back here, press S (See).

The Magical CONTROL-D

CONTROL-D can perform still fancier tricks! You do not have to type the names of existing files. When you are supposed to enter a file name, you can press CONTROL-D instead of typing a name. *MicroWriter* will catalog the disk and display each file name that might be appropriate. This means (a) only text files, not programs, and (b) if you are Writing a file, only unlocked files.

The file names appear one at a time, and the question mark after a displayed name is a reminder that *MicroWriter* is waiting for you to make a decision. To replace a displayed name by another, press any key except CONTROL-D: RETURN is the safest choice. To adopt a displayed name as input, press CONTROL-D yet again.

What happens next varies. If you are Reading or Writing a file, *MicroWriter* will respond immediately and Read or Write the file. If you are entering a DOS command, the only response you will see is that the question mark turns into the usual cursor. *MicroWriter* does not execute a DOS command until you press RETURN. Thus, you can type characters after the file name: you can lengthen the name or add a suffix such as ",D2" or ",New Name". You can even press CONTROL-D yet another time and add another file's name to the command. You can demonstrate these effects as follows:

a. **CONTROL-D** – the entire disk catalog becomes visible, and then press CONTROL-D a second time so that *MicroWriter* will display file names. Notice that the lower display only shows the names of text files. Press RETURN until the cursor reappears, signaling that *MicroWriter* has displayed all of the names. Then press RETURN once more to return here.

b. **CONTROL-R** – Read a file. *MicroWriter* will ask you to name the file. Instead of typing a name, press CONTROL-D, then press RETURN repeatedly until you return here. Note that the locked file Instructions is displayed.

c. **CONTROL-W** – Write a file. First, *MicroWriter* will ask you to specify how the file ends – answer by entering any character that comes after the cursor and pressing RETURN.

(*MicroWriter* will infer that you really intend to record a file. You should have no such intention.) Next, *MicroWriter* will ask you to enter a file name – as before, press CONTROL-D and then press RETURN until you return here. *MicroWriter* will display the name Transfile, which is unlocked, but not the name Instructions, which is locked and so unavailable for Writing. In fact, Transfile might be the only unlocked file on the disk.

d. This time you are going to commit an error so that you will see how harmless this is. Press CONTROL-D to catalog the disk: *MicroWriter* will wait for you to enter a DOS command. Do not enter a command word, just press CONTROL-D and start the sequence of displayed names. Press CONTROL-D a third time while a name is on display. This produces the message SYNTAX ERROR because the entered DOS command did not begin with a legitimate command word such as RENAME or LOCK. After the error message disappears, you will find yourself looking at the editing menu, so press S (See) to come back here. *MicroWriter* displays a menu after any DOS error because that is a way to make sure everything is in order.

e. Enter a legitimate DOS command. First, using a name such as Seg, Write a short segment as an test file. Then, press CONTROL-D to catalog the disk. Type the command word LOCK and then press CONTROL-D again. The file names will appear after the command word. When *MicroWriter* displays the name Seg, press CONTROL-D a third time. This CONTROL-D adds the name Seg to the command, but the command does not execute – *MicroWriter* is waiting for you either to type more characters or to press RETURN. So press RETURN. The new catalog will show that Seg has been locked. Press RETURN to return here.

f. Now for the postgraduate course! RENAME Seg and then delete it from the disk. For example, you could change Seg to Sex. (Renaming requires an unlocked file.)

Like all magicians, CONTROL-D does things behind the scenes. Most of the time, *MicroWriter* puts the file names it is examining into vacant memory space. But when the vacant space in memory falls below 256 characters, *MicroWriter* puts the file names into the wastebasket. Thus, when the memory is nearly full, you should recover text that you want to preserve before you press CONTROL-D.

Finding and Changing Text

CONTROL-F initiates a Find-and-change sequence. When you specify only one string of characters, *MicroWriter* searches for that string. When you specify two strings of characters, *MicroWriter* searches for the first string and replaces it with the second string.

MicroWriter assumes that the very first character in your specification is not a part of the first string but a delimiter. In the reminder *MicroWriter* displays after you press CONTROL-F, this delimiter is a \, but you can use any character as a delimiter. It is best to use an unusual character as a delimiter. The first string continues until this delimiter appears a second time, and the second string continues until the delimiter appears a third time.

If your input includes just two occurrences of a delimiter, *MicroWriter* tries to Find the string you typed between the two delimiters. The following examples would all produce searches for the words "characters sought":

```
\characters sought\
zcharacters soughtz
"characters sought"
^characters sought^second string
```

The last example causes *MicroWriter* to Find but not to change because the second string does not end with a third occurrence of the delimiter ^.

If your specification includes three or more occurrences of a delimiter, *MicroWriter* infers that you want to substitute the string between the second and third occurrences for the string between the first two occurrences. *MicroWriter* ignores any characters you type after the third delimiter. These examples would produce changes:

```
\current string\desired string\
"current string"desired string"
^current string^desired string^ignored third string^
```

You might inadvertently produce some strange results if you forget to begin your input with a delimiter or if you use a prevalent character as a delimiter. The specification:

```
some string\desired string\
```

would cause the words "some string" to become "string\ destring", because *MicroWriter* would infer that you wanted the delimiter to be s. Such mistakes are more often amusing than problematic, however, because they usually generate peculiar sequences of characters that you can readily Find-and-change.

MicroWriter's searches are exact but also narrow-minded. For example, if you tell it to find "supercilious", *MicroWriter* will not find the misspelled "supercillious". If you ask for "he", *MicroWriter* would also find "cheap", "their", and "attached".

You can choose to distinguish between lower-case letters and upper-case ones (capital letters) or to ignore such differences.

You can also cut down on inappropriate matches in two ways. Firstly, include blanks in the strings you specify: to find "the", for instance, it is better to say " the ", so that *MicroWriter* does not also find "other" and "there". Secondly, use the equal sign =. If you include = in the first string you specify, *MicroWriter* interprets it as matching any character. Thus, " =e " matches " he ", " we ", and " be ".

Although = matches any character, it matches only a single character. To match two arbitrary characters, you must type ==.

A disadvantage of using = to represent any character is that you cannot use Find-and-change to locate the equal sign itself. If you press CONTROL-F and then enter the string:

```
\=\
```

MicroWriter will find every character in your text. If you were so foolish as to enter the two strings:

\=\&\

MicroWriter would change every character in your document (in the computer's memory, not on disk) into an ampersand. That just might make you unhappy!

Now, you should practice finding. First, press CONTROL-A to move up to the beginning of these instructions. Then press CONTROL-F and specify that you want to find the string ###. Be sure to add delimiters before and after the three cross-hatches. The first search will end here, and you can stop the search here by pressing any key except RETURN.

Second, start here and find several occurrences of the word "and". Note that the searching begins at the cursor's location when you press CONTROL-F, you do not find the occurrences of "and" above that point.

Third, change "in" to "%%", examine the consequences, then undo these substitutions by changing "%%" back to "in". If your experiments mess up these instructions, you can ESCape to the menu and reread them.

Just Two More

Carriage returns are invisible on the screen, so they can be difficult to discern, yet you may sometimes want to count blank lines or to identify the ends of paragraphs unequivocally. If you press CONTROL-B, *MicroWriter* starts emitting a cheerful little Bell tone whenever the cursor passes a carriage return. Three Bells mean three carriage returns. To turn off this musical accompaniment, press CONTROL-B again. (ESCaping to the menu also turns off the Bell, as do the operations Find-and-change, Transfer, and Write.)

Finally, CONTROL-C induces *MicroWriter* to Count how much vacant space remains in the computer's memory. *MicroWriter's* memory can hold 32,906 characters, which is 128.5 disk sectors.

Since you have now encountered all of the control codes, this would be a good time to press CONTROL-V and review what you have learned.

Oops!

I often hit wrong keys – say, CONTROL-D instead of CONTROL-S – so *MicroWriter* makes it very easy to avoid actions that you initiate by mistake. To abort control actions, you merely press RETURN instead of making appropriate inputs. Suppose that you accidentally press CONTROL-F and initiate a Find-and-change – to abort, press RETURN instead of specifying a string. Similarly, if you press CONTROL-R and then change your mind and decide not to Read, press RETURN.

You can also abort actions by pressing CONTROL-RESET. If you do this in editing mode, *MicroWriter* displays the editing menu, and if you do it in printing mode, *MicroWriter* shows the printing menu.

Beware, however, of pressing CONTROL-RESET while DOS is reading or writing a file – this can leave you with a disk drive that will not turn off until you turn off the computer altogether.

Should you terminate *MicroWriter* by entering the Monitor, and then regret this action, you can reenter *MicroWriter* with:

803G or 2760G

Neither DOS 3.3 nor the Monitor uses the same memory locations as *MicroWriter*. *MicroWriter* does use some of the same locations as Applesoft, and deferred-execution Applesoft programs render *MicroWriter* inoperable. Should you quit *MicroWriter* by entering BASIC, you can reenter *MicroWriter* with:

CALL 2051 or CALL 10080

But you will have to do some tidying up. Mere entry into BASIC always affects the character-spacing parameter in the P (Pick) menu and the left-margin parameter in the S (Start) menu, so you must correct these at least. Applesoft commands might alter other parameters.

Printing

MicroWriter will help you take advantage of your printer. For example, an Epson printer can print in italic font as well as standard font. You can underline one letter, one word, or every word. You can print four sizes of letters, and you can change letter sizes at any point. Thus, you could print one word in enlarged, italic, underlined letters in the middle of a line of pica letters in standard font. You can also print subscripts and superscripts. Printing can be boldfaced by double-striking horizontally or vertically or both.

Alternatively, an Apple DMP can print in ten type sizes with uniform spacing between characters, and in four type sizes with proportional spacing between characters. Printing can be boldfaced by double-striking horizontally, and you can underline anything from one character to an entire document.

The *MicroWriter* disk includes a Printer Test File that you can use to explore your printer's capabilities.

MicroWriter adapts to a very wide range of printers, executing commands that a given printer supports and ignoring commands the printer lacks. The characteristics of a specific printer are described by a block of configuration information within the *MicroWriter* program. The *MicroWriter* disk includes several of these configuration blocks: each block bears the name of a printer. To see the list, catalog the *MicroWriter* disk by pressing CONTROL-D. Assembly-language programmers can create additional configuration blocks.

MicroWriter comes to you configured for an Apple DMP. If you have another printer, you should reconfigure *MicroWriter* now before reading further. T (Terminate) *MicroWriter* and ask for BASIC. Enter these instructions, being careful about capitalization and the two numbers.

```
UNLOCK Microwriter (RETURN)
BLOAD Microwriter (RETURN)
BLOAD Your.Printer (RETURN)
BSAVE Microwriter,A2051,L12882 (RETURN)
LOCK Microwriter (RETURN)
Press Open-Apple, CONTROL, and RESET at the same time.
```

The first BLOAD puts a clean copy of *MicroWriter* into the computer. The second BLOAD superimposes your printer's configuration block on top of the Apple DMP's. "Your.Printer" must, of course, be one of the blocks on the *MicroWriter* disk. The BSAVE records the modified *MicroWriter* program. Be sure you get those numbers right! Pressing Open-Apple, CONTROL, and RESET reloads the revised *MicroWriter*.

Please also set the DIP switches inside your printer to fit your interface card. In particular, most interface cards transmit a linefeed with each carriage return, but some do not: the printer's linefeed switch should be set accordingly.

When it starts, *MicroWriter* assumes that your interface card occupies Slot 1, but you can change this assumption.

Step One: Pick

When beginning to print, your first response to the printing menu should be P for "Pick the Printer's characteristics". This enables you to specify type sizes and fonts. To see these options, (a) turn on your printer, (b) press CONTROL-Q to Quit to printing, and (c) press P in response to the printing menu.

To make a change, first press one of the letters on the left side of the display, then press a letter corresponding to a desired characteristic. Your choice will appear on the right side of the display.

If you ask for a characteristic that your printer lacks (for example, if you ask for proportional spacing from a printer that cannot do it), *MicroWriter* beeps and shows your choice as X. In determining legality, *MicroWriter* may consider combinations of characteristics. For instance, The Apple DMP does proportional spacing with elite or pica letters, but not with other letter sizes. The Epsons print horizontal boldface with pica or enlarged pica letters but not with small or large letters.

You may find the P (Pick) display to be one of *MicroWriter's* non-obvious assets. If you are like me, you tend to forget which combinations work and which do not. Quick-and-dirty experimenting with the P (Pick) display seems easier than reading the printer manual. If you produce Xs that you cannot undo, change the letter size to pica.

When you press RETURN to indicate that the display shows the characteristics you want, *MicroWriter* sends the appropriate signals to the printer. If you forget to turn on your printer before this, *MicroWriter* puts a prompting message on the screen and waits for you to turn on the printer. However, this wait may have an undesirable consequence: the printer may print an extraneous character. Therefore, you should turn on your printer before you accept the printer characteristics.

Because P (Pick) sends signals to the printer immediately, you can use *MicroWriter* to setup your printer for other programs. That is, you can terminate *MicroWriter* after you Pick the Printer's characteristics, and if you do not turn your printer off, it will retain the characteristics that *MicroWriter* gave it.

Within *MicroWriter*, you can override your initial specifications by means of printing codes embedded in your text. However, you should initially press P (Pick) even if your text begins with numerous printing codes, because *MicroWriter* interprets the P (Pick) settings as specifications for page numbers and headings. For instance, if you use P (Pick) to specify small letters and your text begins with an instruction to print large letters, the text prints in large letters and the page headings in small letters.

Step Two: Start

Next, press S to "Start printing on a new page". *MicroWriter* displays format characteristics such as margins, and asks you whether you want to alter anything.

The top margin begins below the page number, if any. Page numbers and headings always print on line 2.

The widths of the left and right margins depend upon the sizes of letters as well as on the numbers of columns. A margin 6 columns wide would be .6 of an inch with pica letters (10 per inch), but 6 columns would be 1.2 inches if the letters are enlarged Pica (5 per inch).

You should pay attention to the left and right margins shown in the S (Start) display even if your text begins with margin specifications: the displayed margins determine the left-to-right placement of page numbers and headings.

MicroWriter ignores the spaces you insert into your text to indent the first lines of paragraphs, and instead, indents the first lines of paragraphs according to the indent number you specify when starting printing. Thus, even though the paragraphs in these instructions begin with five spaces, you could print the instructions indented seven spaces or no spaces. (You can alter the indent number via printing codes in your text.)

```
Outdenting is the inverse of
        indenting. This paragraph is
        outdented five spaces: the first
        line begins five spaces to the
        left of the subsequent lines.
        Outdenting offers a good way to
        print in outline form -- like
        this:
I. A major heading and some text that
        goes with it.
        A. A secondary heading and
           text that goes with it.
           1. A tertiary heading and
              still more text.
To outdent, tell MicroWriter that you
        want to indent more than 127
        spaces. The outdent will be 256
        minus the number you specify. For
        instance, to outdent 5 spaces,
        you would say that you want to
        indent 251. To outdent 9 spaces,
        you would specify an indent of
        247 because
              256 - 9 = 247.
Outdenting works like this because the
        computer perceives outdenting as
        indenting with negative numbers.
        According to the odd logic of a
        microcomputer, 256 is the same as
        zero, 255 equals -1, 254 equals
        -2, and so on. Thus, 251 = -5,
        and 247 = -9.
```

```
Being negative indentations, outdented
        lines protrude to the left of the
        official left margin. You must
        set the left margin far enough
        right to allow for the protruding
        lines. The left margin minus the
        outdent defines the left end of
        outdented lines, and you have to
        make the left margin big enough
        that outdented lines start in
        column 1 or higher.
Another way to state the foregoing
        rule is to say that, when
        outdenting, the left margin
        plus the indent number must add
        to 257 or more. If they sum to
        257, the outdented lines begin in
        column 1. If they add to 265, the
        outdented lines begin in column
        8.
```

To single-space, tell *MicroWriter* to space 1 between text lines. To double-space, tell *MicroWriter* to space 2. And so on.

MicroWriter never numbers page 1: page numbering begins with page 2. You can number page 1 manually by typing a center-justified "Page 1" at the beginning of your text. *MicroWriter* also prints no heading on page 1, but you can type a center-justified heading at the start of your text. *MicroWriter* will print a heading on every page if you make the first page number zero.

You can save paper by previewing text before you print it. The S (Start) display lets you choose to preview at slow speed, to preview at high speed, or to print on paper. Previewing proceeds rather briskly even at slow speed, so you may want to keep a finger on a key. Any key will do except ESC – the space bar has the virtues of being large and central. When you touch a key, the previewing or printing halts until you touch a key again. If you touch a key twice in quick succession, the first touch will restart the printing and the second touch will halt the printing almost immediately – at the end of the next printed line. Thus, you can step through your text one line at a time.

Although you can press a key to halt printing at any time, *MicroWriter* finishes printing a complete line before it halts. This simplifies the tasks involved in interrupting and resuming printing. It also recognizes the practicality that printing occurs too quickly for people to regulate printing one-word-at-a-time.

If your computer has an 80-column text card, *MicroWriter* activates this card for previewing (but not for printing on paper). An 80-column display does a much better job of portraying a printed page than does the normal 40-column display. A 40-column display means that each printed line of 80 characters takes up two lines on the screen.

When previewing, *MicroWriter* stops at the end of the file and waits for you to press a key.

One minor and rare difference between the previewed text on screen and the actual text on paper arises with lines that end in the same column as the screen's width – for example, with lines that end in column 80 on an 80-column screen. Such lines occur mainly with right-justified text when the right margin is in column 80. These lines appear to be double-spaced on screen even though they are single-spaced on paper.

A Superficial Encounter

You should now try some previewing. After you read this section of the instructions, press CONTROL-Q to Quit to printing. When you see the printing menu, press B for "Backup to the Beginning of the file". This assures that printing will start at the beginning of these instructions. Next, press P (Pick), and after you complete that operation, press S (Start).

Tell *MicroWriter* to preview Slowly. You can stop this previewing temporarily by pressing any key. When you then press a key other than ESC, the previewing resumes. Try that a few times, then take note of the last words printed and press ESC to exit.

Pressing ESC makes *MicroWriter* display the printing menu. Press Q to "Quit to editing" and then S (See). Observe the cursor's location – it should be just to the right of the last words printed.

Also notice how the printing mode treats the lines above that look outdented in editing mode. The truth is that these lines are not outdented – the text includes no such printing code, and *MicroWriter* does not outdent in editing mode. I have created the appearance of outdenting by making each line a separate paragraph, and TABbing before most of these paragraphs. (To verify that each of these lines is a separate paragraph, shift into editing mode and turn on the Bell with CONTROL-B.) In printing mode, *MicroWriter* first strips all of the blanks off the beginnings of these lines, and then indents each line the amount specified for a paragraph. Thus, every line ends up indented the same distance.

Mixing It Up

The cursor plays an important role in printing as well as editing. The next characters to be printed are the ones just to the cursor's right. If you Quit to the printing menu from here, printing will begin at the cursor's present location. If you then print only a few lines and return to editing, the cursor will have moved to the point where you stopped printing. This allows you to mix editing with printing. But it also makes you responsible for the cursor's location when printing begins. To start printing at the beginning of a document, you have to put the cursor at the document's beginning. You can do this in two ways: either press CONTROL-A before you Quit to printing, or press B (Backup) in response to the printing menu.

When you press S (Start), *MicroWriter* acts as if printing is starting at the top of a new page. This might not be page 1: it could be page 35 if you state that page number. You can also determine whether the first line on this new page ought to be indented as the start of a paragraph.

Unless you specify that the first page number is zero, the first page number changes as printing proceeds. Just after page 1 has begun, the first page number is 2: if you stop the printing before the end of page 1, press ESC to go to the menu, and press S (Start), the printing will start at the top of page 2. Because the first page number does change, you have to reset it to 1 whenever you want to start printing at page 1.

If you have printed part of a page and you do not want to start a new page but to resume with the next line on the same page, you should press C to "Continue printing on the same page". C (Continue) resumes with the previous printer characteristics, format, and page number. Again, you can choose whether the first line printed is indented.

You can use C (Continue) to print very long documents. Suppose hypothetically that you wanted to print the files making up these instructions. You should press P (Pick) and S (Start) when beginning to print the first file, Instructions. After that file has been printed, you would see the printing menu again: you should respond by pressing R (Read) to read Instructions 2, and then press C (Continue). You need not press B (Backup) after reading the second file because reading via a menu leaves the cursor at the beginning of the file. After the second file has been printed, you should read Instructions 3 and again press C (Continue). (Do not try to print Instructions 3 yet, because this file includes printing codes that would drive your printer crazy. I will explain how to print Instructions 3 later.)

Suppose you wanted to print these instructions but to delete the final paragraphs that tell you to read the next file: you should Quit to editing before you print the first two files. In this case, you would have to move the cursor to the beginning of each file after you edit it and before you print it.

Because *MicroWriter* insists that C (Continue) start a new line, each file making up a long document should end with a complete line or paragraph.

When you finish printing a document and you want to advance the paper to the top of the next sheet, press F for "Formfeed to top of Form".

The menu for printing also includes "E = Erase the printer's buffer". What this does varies among printers. On some printers (Apple and C.Itoh), it deletes characters but leaves the printing format unchanged. On other printers (Epson and Panasonic), it restores the printer to the pristine state it had when you first turned it on. You can also achieve the latter result by manually turning a printer off and on again.

A Less Superficial Encounter

Try shifting back and forth between editing and printing. Convince yourself that *MicroWriter* will start and stop printing where you say. Also, experiment with diverse formats such as wide versus narrow margins, single versus triple spacing, different kinds of indentation. To save paper, you should run most of these experiments via previewing, but do also try printing on paper.

You will get weird results if you try to print the section titled "All the Codes That Are Fit To Print". That section describes the printing codes, and *MicroWriter* will execute each printing code. The text above that point amounts to about three single-spaced pages. If you want to practice on a long section of text, Read Instructions or Instructions 2 again – these include no printing codes.

Printing Codes in the Text

The P (Pick) and S (Start) displays give you quick, simple means of printing. At first, you may prefer to do only what those displays permit. You do not have to imbed printing codes within your text. But these codes are the main keys to *MicroWriter's* printing versatility.

Press CONTROL-V again and briefly survey the four help displays that list printing codes. Note that each code begins with an exclamation mark, followed by two lower-case letters. The second letter is a generic category – m for margin, j for justify, b for boldface, l for letters. In some codes but not all, numbers follow the letters.

When *MicroWriter* encounters an exclamation mark during printing, it compares the next two characters with the list of printing codes. If a match occurs, *MicroWriter* changes the printing format or the printer's characteristics. Then *MicroWriter* assumes that you might have added a comment that you do not want printed: *MicroWriter* does not resume printing after a printing code until after it encounters another exclamation mark or a carriage return. Thus, you can insert reminders to yourself. If you want to insert a reminder but you do not want to change anything, use the code !cm (for comment) – this code does nothing to the printer or the format.

Should You End with an Exclamation?

Printing codes must end with either exclamation marks or carriage returns, and it matters which you use. Suppose that you want to specify several format or printer characteristics at once. You can say something like this:

```
!lj
!lm7
!rm73
!in5
```

The above code sequence says left justify, put the left margin in column 7 and the right margin in column 73, and indent the first line of each paragraph 5 spaces. Each printing code ends with a carriage return, but *MicroWriter* does not print these carriage returns because they come right after printing codes. Since neither the printing codes nor the carriage returns are printed, these lines become invisible.

It makes sense to chain related codes together into a single statement. You can chain codes by ending each code with an exclamation mark – like this:

```
!lj!!lm7!!rm73!!in5
```

The left-justify code, the left-margin code, and the right-margin code end with exclamation marks – only the indent code ends with a carriage return. In writing these compound sequences, you use exclamation marks much like parentheses – the exclamation marks enclose the letters and numbers. You could also add comments:

```
!lj!!lm7!!rm73!!in5 Comment
                 or
!lj Comment !!lm7!!rm73!!in5
```

Printing codes that come after and end with carriage returns stand out like separate paragraphs. This makes them easy to see, but it also prevents you from making format or printing changes within paragraphs. Therefore, you need not end a code sequence with a carriage return. If you end a code sequence with an exclamation mark, *MicroWriter* will resume printing with the character immediately following the exclamation mark. In this example, the name "Ajax" would be underlined, the word "doubled" would be in italic font, and the rest of the sentence would print in standard font without underlining:

```
!sf!!nu!During the next six years, !ul!Ajax!nu! more
than !if!doubled!sf! its profits.
```

Indeed, you can insert printing codes into the middle of a word. This sentence, for instance, wo!hdStill More Instructions!!in7!uld change the heading and the amount of indenting.

Printing codes that end with exclamation marks also enable you to force spaces at the left end of a line. To make sure that left margins and paragraph indents fit your specifications, *MicroWriter* starts each printed line by removing any blank spaces at that point in your text. But you might want to circumvent this action. You can do so by beginning the line with any printing code, like this:

```
!cm!   This line starts with 3 spaces.
```

When you mix text and printing codes within a paragraph, it is good practice to end every code with an exclamation mark, including a code that ends the paragraph. Suppose that you typed:

```
!in0!Flush-left Heading!in5
```

Because the last characters in the line are a printing code, *MicroWriter* infers that you do not want it to print the carriage return after !in5. Thus, no carriage return follows this heading – which is probably not what you intended. You will get what you want by saying:
```
!in0!Flush-left Heading!in5!
```

All the Codes That Are Fit To Print

You may not need explanations for more than a couple of the printing codes, but to play it safe, here is a complete list. The following codes do not depend upon the capabilities of specific printers:

!tm2   Make the top margin 2 lines long.

!bm8   Make the bottom margin 8 lines long, at least (perhaps longer if there are blank lines between printed lines).

!lm7   Begin text in column 7, end left margin in column 6.

!rm74   End text in column 74, begin right margin in column 75

!cj   Center justify each line between the left and right margins. *MicroWriter* center justifies all page numbers and headings.

!rj   Right justify each line and make a straight right margin. Right justify works poorly with proportional spacing, because *MicroWriter* assumes that every character has the same width.

!lj   Left justify each line and create a straight left margin.

MicroWriter does not fully justify (that is, create straight margins at both the left and the right simultaneously). Simple schemes for doing this insert irregular spaces between words – these look ugly and they slow down reading. Schemes that produce equal spaces between words are pretty complex:

!sp2   Double-space lines of text.

!pg24   Make the next page number 24.

!hd My Swan Song   Make the page heading "My Swan Song". Headings must be less than 64 characters long and narrow enough to fit between the left and right margins at the time it is entered.

!lp66   Make each page 66 lines long.

!np   Issue a formfeed and start a new page.

!in5   Indent first line following each carriage return 5 spaces.

!cm   Comment only.

!pcABCD   Transmit the characters ABCD to the printer: ABCD should be a printer-control code. To transmit a control character per se (that is, a character with an ASCII number below 32), place a ^ in front of a corresponding letter, number, punctuation mark, or special character. Thus, ^H or ^h or ^(would transmit an 8 (BS), and ^[or ^{ or ^; would transmit a 27 (ESC).

MicroWriter also recognizes these instructions for printers. No printer can execute all combinations of these:

!bs3   Backspace three spaces. Backspacing enables you to overstrike previously printed characters.

!bs   The backspace code with no number produces a single backspace: !bs = !bs1. With lower-case letters, a backspace followed by a quotation mark can simulate an umlaut.

!sh   Short-height lines, typically 1/8th of an inch. Apple and C.Itoh call this linefeed pitch.

!nh   Normal-height lines, 1/6th of an inch.

!vb   Vertical boldface. Strike each line a second time, after rolling the paper a fraction of an inch vertically. Epson calls this double striking, Mannesmann calls it correspondence quality, and Panasonic calls it double printing.

!hb   Horizontal boldface. Strike each dot a second time, after moving the print head a fraction of an inch horizontally. Several manufacturers call this emphasized printing.

!db   Double boldface. Strike each dot four times, both twice horizontally and twice vertically.

!nb	Not boldface. Strike each dot once. Mannesmann calls this draft mode.
!if	Print in italic font.
!af	Print in alternate font. On most printers, I used this for the British character set.
!sf	Print in standard font.
!ps	Start proportional spacing between characters.
!us	Start uniform spacing between characters, stop proportional spacing.

With some printers (Apple DMP, C.Itoh), you must specify a letter size after you change from uniform spacing to proportional spacing, or vice versa:

!ul	Start to underline characters and spaces.
!nu	No underlining or stop underlining.
!vl	Print with very small letters. 17/inch on the Apple DMP. 20/inch on the Mannesmann.
!sl	Print with small letters. 15/inch on the Apple DMP. 16.7/inch on the Mannesmann. 17/inch on the C.Itoh. 17.13/inch on the Epsons.
!el	Print with elite letters, 12 per inch.
!pl	Print with pica letters, 10 per inch.
!ll	Print with large letters. 9/inch on the Apple DMP. 8.5/inch on the Epsons.

Most printers can enlarge characters. Apple calls this headline type, Epson calls it double-width or enlarged type, C.Itoh and Panasonic call it elongated type. *MicroWriter's* printing codes resemble those for normal letters but the first letters are capitalized:

!Vl   Print with enlarged very small letters.
        8.5/inch on the Apple DMP.
        10/inch on the Mannesmann.

!Sl   Print with enlarged small letters.
        7.5/inch on the Apple DMP.
        8.3/inch on the Mannesmann.
        8.5/inch on the Epsons and the C.Itoh.

!El   Print with enlarged elite letters, 6 per inch.

!Pl   Print with enlarged pica letters, 5 per inch.

!Ll   Print with enlarged large letters.
        4.5/inch on the Apple DMP.
        5/inch on the Epsons.

!ht   Print as high, tiny superscripts.

!lt   Print as low, tiny subscripts.

!qt   Quit printing as superscripts or subscripts.

Sampling the Wares

This sample of text illustrates various uses of the printing codes:

```
!sp2!!sf!!us!!pl!!pg0!!lm50!!in0!!rm73
Camp Hiawatha
Aching Back, Wisconsin
July 4, 2001

!lm7
Dear Mom,

!in5
```

```
My group leader !if!hates!sf! me, and my
roommate, Alice, wets his bed. The food is
!ul!!if!horrible!!nu!!sf! They're trying to
!Pl!poison!pl! us.
!cm That should get her sympathy.
Alice won the ping-pong tournament.
We played a baseball game with Camp Gitchee-Gumee. They
cheated, and the umpire was on their side, so we lost
!cj
24-0,
!lj!!in0
almost as badly as last year.
!rm66!!lm6!!in4!!ll
Send money.!pl!!lm7!!rm73! I want to buy you the
!ul!Camp Hiawatha Cookbook!nu! for a present. !cm How
could this miss?! Also, send me some fudge brownies with
marshmallows in them. !if!!hb!Please.

!sf!!nb!!rj
Love,
!rm37!!if!!hb!!Pl
Henry
!sf!!nb!!pl!!rm73!!lj!!in0

P.S. Can I come back here again next year?
```

A Truly Meaningful Encounter

Try printing the sample letter. It shows some of your printer's versatility. By properly locating the cursor, you should be able to print the letter without also printing the text that precedes it. You may find it difficult to halt the printing after the postscript and before the row of asterisks. To make halting easy, you can:

1. Insert the new-page code !np! below the postscript and above the row of asterisks.

2. Tell *MicroWriter* to pause at the start of a new page.

3. When *MicroWriter* pauses, press CONTROL-RESET to abort the printing.

Goofed Again!

MicroWriter checks your format and printer specifications and modifies or ignores any improper ones. Suppose that you have been printing with pica letters with 80 characters per line. You decide to shift to printing with large letters, so you press P (Pick) and make this change. Then you press S (Start). *MicroWriter* reports that a margin specification has been modified: because there cannot be 80 large letters per line, *MicroWriter* has reduced the right margin.

Similarly, you may hear a bell and see an error message while *MicroWriter* is printing your text. You should take this as a recommendation to check your printing codes at that point in the text: although *MicroWriter* proceeds, the results might not be what you want.

There are, however, important differences between *MicroWriter's* checks with the P (Pick) and S (Start) displays and its checks during printing. As the above example shows, at the start of printing, *MicroWriter* verifies that the right margin is consistent with the sizes of letters. During printing, *MicroWriter* lets you alter the sizes of letters without checking the right margin. This permits you to mix larger and smaller letters within a single line, but it also allows you to make mistakes that *MicroWriter* does not prevent. For example, my initial attempt at the Camp Hiawatha letter caused "Send money." to occupy a line by itself, because my printing codes made the printer unhappy.

MicroWriter does not set the printer's characteristics to X in response to printing codes in the text. It allows you to set the characteristics to illegal values, but then refuses to transmit the illegal codes to the printer. These rules may save you a few headaches:

1. Shift the left and right margins to fit the larger letters before you increase letter sizes. For example:

   ```
   !lm6!!rm60!!ll
   ```

2. But decrease letter sizes before you shift the left and right margins to fit the smaller letters. For example:

```
!pl!!lm7!!rm73
```

3. Move the left margin right before you start to outdent or before you increase the outdent distance. For example:

```
!lm13!!in250
```

4. But when you stop outdenting or decrease the outdent distance, change the outdent number before you try to move the left margin left. For example:

```
!in5!!lm7
```

5. Shift to proportional or uniform spacing before specifying an appropriate letter size. For example:

```
!ps!!el
!us!!Vl
```

You can use the P (Pick) display to test the legality of code sequences. And you can use the S (Start) display to find the maximum numbers of characters per line with various letter sizes – just enter a right margin, such as 240, that you know to be too large.

Epxon RX-80?

Every printer has peculiarities, but the Epson RX-80 has driven me up the wall. This printer seems to work just fine most of the time. But when single spacing, it reacts weirdly if lines begin with printing codes that send signals to the printer – it prints such lines on top of the preceding lines. Epson would not let me to talk to an engineer, referring me instead to their distributor, who cannot answer my questions.

After much experimenting work, I have concluded that the RX-80 has defective firmware. But do not despair if you own an RX-80 – you can force the missing linefeeds by putting !pc^*! in front of any printing codes that cause problems.

Casting Spells

MicroWriter works just fine with a spelling checker such as *Sensible Speller*. You should tell your spelling checker not to ignore any lines. Do not tell it to ignore lines that begin with an exclamation mark, because such lines may include text as well as printing codes. If your spelling checker insists upon your naming a character that begins a line to ignore, tell it to ignore lines that begin with CONTROL-Q, which never occurs in a *MicroWriter* file.

To keep printing codes from popping up as misspelled words, add the codes to your dictionary. The *MicroWriter* disk includes a file, Printing Codes for Dictionary, that lists most of the codes likely to occur. Add these to your dictionary. Should you frequently use a code I left out, just add it to your dictionary as well.

To keep your spelling checker from getting confused, you should begin every comment in the printing codes with a blank space: !cm Comment! instead of !cmComment!. The same practice works with new headings as well, but a space at the start of a heading may cause the heading to be printed one character to the right of center.

Better Tailoring Than Savile Row

The two hello programs offer you several means of adapting *MicroWriter* for different uses or your personal preferences. The short program named Hello initiates a longer program named More Hello. Both programs include REM statements pointing out options. I recommend that you use an aid such as the Program Line Editor when changing these programs. You should also make any changes on copies of the *MicroWriter* disk, not on the original disk.

In particular, once you learn to use *MicroWriter*, you should consider changing the initial file name from Instructions to something else. On a disk titled "Correspondence", for example, you could record your letterhead and the general outlines of a letter under the file name "Form", and then you could have *MicroWriter* ask initially if you want to read Form. The numeric codes for Form are 198, 239, 242, 237, 141.

The initial file name comprises line 190 of More Hello. When changing this initial file name, you must neither increase nor decrease the number of characters from the present count (30). Use carriage returns (141) to fill up the spaces that you do not want to use for the name itself. When you change the initial file name, you will want to modify as well the display produced by lines 140, 150, and 160. Other tailoring options may be less useful to you.

Hello moves DOS 3.3 into the bank-switched memory in order to gain about 10,000 more spaces for your text. But *MicroWriter* can operate equally well with DOS in its usual location. You might want to keep DOS out of the bank-switched memory if, for example, you intend to use *MicroWriter* only to setup the printer and then you intend to run a program that depends upon DOS occupying its usual location. To make this change, just modify line 40 of Hello, as indicated there.

In More Hello, line 200 defines the cursor: you can replace the flashing square with any inverse or flashing character that suits your fancy, except inverse @. *MicroWriter* interprets the ASCII code zero (which would normally produce an inverse @) as indicating that you want the cursor to be a speckled square.

Line 210 specifies whether you want to see 40 columns or 80 when *MicroWriter* begins. Your computer must contain an 80-column card in order for *MicroWriter* to display 80 columns.

Line 220 defines the symbol that begins and usually ends printing codes. If you object to exclamation marks, you can begin and end printing codes with any ordinary (not inverse, not flashing, not control) character. This character should be one that occurs infrequently in text because *MicroWriter* tests for a possible printing code every time it encounters the character – a period, comma, or quotation mark would be a poor choice. An letter might result in fragments of text being mistaken for printing codes, as might a character, such as a hyphen or left parenthesis, that could precede letters. The printing-code symbol should also be a character, such as a colon or right parenthesis, that your spelling checker identifies as coming after a word. You doubtless see the advantages of an exclamation mark.

Of course, you can change the number of spaces to TAB via CONTROL-N, but this number is set initially in line 230.

Line 240 specifies the slot occupied by the printer-interface card.

With most printer-interface cards, the codes to configure the printer (for example, to change letter sizes) do not appear on screen during printing. Lines 250 to 370 examine the printer-interface card and classify it as resembling a familiar card. If *MicroWriter* produces very strange effects, bad assumptions about the interface card are the most likely reasons. In that event, you should read the file named About Machine Language and the REMs in More Hello.

Printing the Manual

While A.P.P.L.E. sells the *MicroWriter* manual you are reading, you can also print the original instructions on disk. If you choose to print them yourself, you can print Instructions and Instructions 2 without modifying *MicroWriter*, but you must change the printing-code symbol in order to print Instructions 3 without *MicroWriter's* executing the various printing codes.

You can change the printing-code symbol temporarily without altering More Hello. ESCape to the menu, press T (Terminate), and choose M (Monitor). Then type (including the space between C and N):

```
8:FC N803G (RETURN)
```

This makes the printing-code symbol a vertical bar. You can verify the change by Viewing the help displays. Now when *MicroWriter* encounters !np! or any other characters beginning with an exclamation mark, the characters have no special significance.

Before printing the instructions, you may want to go through them first and insert a few printing codes using the new symbol |. For example, the display of CONTROL-J and CONTROL-K near the beginning of Instructions needs a |cm| to make the arrows line up correctly. Also, the section of Instructions 2 that looks outdented on the screen has no printing codes whatever – you could insert left-margin commands to indent the secondary lines. To see what needs fixing, preview the files.

The *MicroWriter* disk includes an index to the instructions. This index included on the disk assumes that you printed the instructions with a pica type, that you used the margin settings that appear in the S (Start) display when *MicroWriter* initiates, and that you deleted nothing and inserted two blank lines after each instructions file.

To change the printing-code symbol back to an exclamation mark, exit to the Monitor and enter:

```
8:A1 N803G (RETURN)
```

You can also print the help displays:

1. Turn on the printer.

2. Use P (Pick) to choose the printer characteristics.

3. Press T (Terminate) and then B (BASIC).

4. Enter: `PR#1 (RETURN)`
            `CALL 2051 (RETURN)`

5. Switch the printer off-line and press the formfeed button to start a new page, then switch the printer back online.

6. Press V (View).

7. Use the RETURN key to change displays. Also, you may want to switch the printer off-line and insert some linefeeds or formfeeds between the displays and after the sixth display.

8. After the help displays end, again press T (Terminate) and then B (BASIC).

9. Enter: `PR#0 (RETURN)`
            `CALL 2051 (RETURN)`

All Work and No Play

A working copy of the *MicroWriter* disk must include only five files: *Hello, Identifier, DOS Mover, More Hello*, and *MicroWriter*.

To Assembly Language Programmers

The *MicroWriter* disk includes the assembly language source code for a typical printer-configuration block. That sample contains explanatory comments. With an assembler such as *Big Mac*, you can alter the provided configurations, and you can create configuration blocks for additional printers. The code transmitted for each printing code can be up to 8 bytes long.

If you see some way to improve a configuration block, or if you create a block for another printer, please contact A.P.P.L.E.. It is also possible to adapt *MicroWriter* to drive a serial card or modem.

Memory Usage

```
Zero page (some of it)
      Cursor symbol                            $06
      How many columns to show                 $07
      Printing-code symbol                     $08
      End of text                        $1B-$1C
      Format parameters                  $7E-$8F
      TABbing number                           $CF
      Printer interface       $D0-$D5,$D7,$DA
      Is there an 80-column card?              $EB
      Start of vacant space              $EC-$ED
      End of vacant space                $EE-$EF

MicroWriter per se                  $0803-$3877
      The editor                    $0803-$275F
      The printer                   $2760-$389F
            (Both $803 and $2760 are entry points)

Configuration block                 $38A0-$3A15
The heading                         $3A16-$3A54
The active file name                $3A55-$3A72
Start-of-text code (03)                   $3A73
First character or cursor                 $3A74
```

The initial format parameters are stored in the same space as the heading.

43

The cursor represents vacant space in the middle of the text, so the cursor symbol has two locations that change often – where the vacant space begins and where it ends. Its lower location is stored in $EC-$ED, and its upper location in $EE-$EF.

End of text with DOS low (03) $91FF
End of text with DOS high (03) $BAFF
The location of the end of text is stored in $1B-$1C.

The wastebasket follows the text and ends four pages higher, $9200-$95FF or $BB00-$BEFF.

With DOS high, $BF00-$BFFF contains the DOS transfer information. $BFFC-$BFFF hold the length (L) and origin (A) of a recently processed file.

The routine at $2C66-78 transmits codes to a printer. With most interface cards, this routine looks like:

```
2C66-   PHA
2C67-   LDA $C1C1
2C6A-   AND $D3
2C6C-   BNE $2C67
2C6E-   PLA
2C6F-   STA $C090
2C72-   RTS
```

$2C73-$2C78 is not used and location $D3 contains $80. Thus, instead of outputting a code character via COUT, *MicroWriter* waits until $C1C1 turns positive and then stores the character in $C090.

The code at $2C66-78 is flexible. The More Hello program pokes data into $D2-$D5, $D7, and $DA, then the code at $2782-CC uses these data to rewrite $2C66-78.

If $D2 <> 0, the code at $2793-A9 and $27B7-CC computes the addresses in $2C70-77, and writes the address in $2C68-69 and the branch instruction in $2C6C. Thus, with a Skyman card in Slot 2, the routine might become:

```
2C66-    PHA
2C67-    LDA $C0AD
2C6A-    AND $D3
2C6C-    BNE $2C67
2C6E-    PLA
2C6F-    STA $C0A0
2C72-    RTS
```

where $D3 holds $10. $2C72 holds RTS unless the interface card is a Dumpling GX ($DA $\diamond$ 0).

If $D2 = 0, the code at $27AA-B6 puts JMP COUT into $2C66-68. In this event, printer codes appear on the screen during printing. COUT can work with every interface card, but you will probably have to revise the printer configuration block by converting $1B to $9B, $53 to $D3, and so on. Output through COUT is necessary for an Interactive Structures EP12G or an Apple Super Serial card, for instance, because writing data directly into these cards requires a much more elaborate routine than *MicroWriter* offers.

```
* This is the configuration block for the Apple DMP.
* Copyright 1984 by Bill Starbuck

        ORG $38A0

*The code table contains the codes to be transmitted to the
*    printer. Fill unused bytes with FF: MicroWriter stops
*    sending when it encounters an FF.

*MicroWriter prefixes every code with a null character
*    because printers sometimes fail to react to codes
*    unless they get such warnings. If you want to stop
*    this, modify the More Hello program.

*The uniform-spacing and proportional-spacing codes are
*    transmitted immediately and then repeated as prefixes
*    to subsequent letter-size codes. The nulls in us and
*    ps tell MicroWriter not to ignore the !us and !ps codes
```

```
              HEX 00FFFFFFFFFFFFFF ;us
              HEX 00FFFFFFFFFFFFFF ;ps
              HEX 9B41FFFFFFFFFFFF ;nh
              HEX 9B42FFFFFFFFFFFF ;sh
              HEX 9B59FFFFFFFFFFFF ;nu
              HEX 9B58FFFFFFFFFFFF ;ul
              HEX 9B5A25529B442252 ;sf
              HEX FFFFFFFFFFFFFFFF ;if
              HEX 9B5A24529B442352 ;af
              HEX 9B22FFFFFFFFFFFF ;nb
              HEX FFFFFFFFFFFFFFFF ;vb
              HEX 9B21FFFFFFFFFFFF ;hb
              HEX FFFFFFFFFFFFFFFF ;db
              HEX FFFFFFFFFFFFFFFF ;ht
              HEX FFFFFFFFFFFFFFFF ;lt
              HEX FFFFFFFFFFFFFFFF ;qt
              HEX 0F9B51FFFFFFFFFF ;vl
              HEX 0F9B71FFFFFFFFFF ;sl
              HEX 0F9B45FFFFFFFFFF ;el
              HEX 0F9B4EFFFFFFFFFF ;pl
              HEX 0F9B6EFFFFFFFFFF ;ll
              HEX 0E9B51FFFFFFFFFF ;Vl
              HEX 0E9B71FFFFFFFFFF ;Sl
              HEX 0E9B45FFFFFFFFFF ;El
              HEX 0E9B4EFFFFFFFFFF ;Pl
              HEX 0E9B6EFFFFFFFFFF ;Ll
              HEX 18FFFFFFFFFFFFFF ;erase the printer's buffer
LINPG         HEX FF42FFFFFFFFFFFF ;set lines/page

*For a printer that lacks a lines/page code, set LINPG
*   = FF and set LINPG+1 = lines/page (66 = $42), as
*   in this example. If LINPG <> FF, MicroWriter sends the
*   code and then sends the number of lines in the S=Start
*   display.

              HEX FFFFFFFFFFFFFFFF ;v proportional
              HEX FFFFFFFFFFFFFFFF ;s proportional
              HEX 0F9B50FFFFFFFFFF ;e proportional
              HEX 0F9B70FFFFFFFFFF ;p proportional
              HEX FFFFFFFFFFFFFFFF ;l proportional
              HEX FFFFFFFFFFFFFFFF ;V proportional
              HEX FFFFFFFFFFFFFFFF ;S proportional
              HEX 0E9B50FFFFFFFFFF ;E proportional
              HEX 0E9B70FFFFFFFFFF ;P proportional
              HEX FFFFFFFFFFFFFFFF ;L proportional
```

```
*The can-do table shows legal combinations of letter
*    sizes, proportional or uniform spacing, and boldfacing.
*    1s denote legal, 0s denote illegal.
*    The left 4 bits = uniform spacing, and
*    the right 4 = proportional spacing.
*    In each group, the 4 bits (from left to right)
*    represent nb,vb,hb,db.

          HEX A0          ;v
          HEX A0          ;s
          HEX AA          ;e
          HEX AA          ;p
          HEX A0          ;l
          HEX A0          ;V
          HEX A0          ;S
          HEX AA          ;E
          HEX AA          ;P
          HEX A0          ;L


*This list states the numbers of characters per line.

          HEX 88          ;v = 136
          HEX 78          ;s = 120
          HEX 60          ;e = 96
          HEX 50          ;p = 80
          HEX 48          ;l = 72
          HEX 44          ;V = 68
          HEX 3C          ;S = 60
          HEX 30          ;E = 48
          HEX 28          ;P = 40
          HEX 24          ;L = 36
          HEX 00          ;v proportional
          HEX 00          ;s proportional
          HEX 78          ;e = 120 proportional
          HEX 6C          ;p = 108 proportional
          HEX 00          ;l proportional
          HEX 00          ;V proportional
          HEX 00          ;S proportional
          HEX 3C          ;E = 60 proportional
          HEX 36          ;P = 54 proportional
          HEX 00          ;L proportional
```

```
*The letter-size list gives the widths of characters. These
*  are 65536 divided by the numbers of characters per line.
*  Thus, 65536/80 = 819.2 = $333.  Including this table
*  saves the space that a division routine would require.


          HEX 01E2          ;v
          HEX 0222          ;s
          HEX 02AB          ;e
          HEX 0333          ;p
          HEX 038E          ;l
          HEX 03C4          ;V
          HEX 0444          ;S
          HEX 0555          ;E
          HEX 0666          ;P
          HEX 071D          ;L
          HEX FFFF          ;v proportional
          HEX FFFF          ;s proportional
          HEX 0222          ;e proportional
          HEX 025F          ;p proportional
          HEX FFFF          ;l proportional
          HEX FFFF          ;V proportional
          HEX FFFF          ;S proportional
          HEX 0444          ;E proportional
          HEX 04BE          ;P proportional
          HEX FFFF          ;L proportional
```

Quick Reference

Main Menu (Editing Menu)

C	=	Clear memory and start a new file
S	=	See the text that is in memory
R	=	Read a file from disk
W	=	Write a file onto disk
DELETE	=	Delete a file from disk
D	=	Catalog and issue Disk commands
E	=	Exchange disk drives
Q	=	Quit to printing
V	=	View the help displays
A	=	Alter the columns displayed
T	=	Terminate MicroWriter

Printing Menu

P	=	Pick the Printer's characteristics
S	=	Start printing on a new page
C	=	Continue printing on the same page
B	=	Backup to the Beginning of the file
R	=	Read a file from disk
F	=	Form feed to top of Form
E	=	Erase the printer's buffer
Q	=	Quit to editing
T	=	Terminate MicroWriter

CONTROL Codes − Left side of Keyboard

ESC = Escape to Menu

TAB = Insert Blanks

Q = Quit to Print Menu

W = Write

E = Exchange

R = Read

T = Transfer

Y = Recover 256 Characters

A = To Beginning of Document

S = Up Many (about 12 lines)

D = Disk

F = Find

G = Get One Character

H = Back (or Left Arrow)

Z = To End of Document

X = Down Many (about 12 lines)

C = Count Spaces

V = View Help Screens

B = Bell

N = Number to Tab

CONTROL Codes – Right side of Keyboard

U	=	Forward (or Right Arrow)
I	=	Tab Insert Blanks
O	=	Delete One Word
P	=	Delete One Paragraph
[	=	ESCape to Menu
]	=	Delete One Word
/	=	Delete One Paragraph
J	=	V (Down)
K	=	^ (Up)
L	=	Delete One Character
DELETE	=	Delete One Character
M	=	Return

Printer Characteristics – Defaults

A = Character Spacing:
  U=Uniform, P=Proportional   U

B = Line Height:
  N=Normal, S=Short   N

C = Underlining:
  N=No, U=Underline   N

D = Font:
  S=Standard, I = Italic, A =Alternate   S

E = Boldface:
  N=No, H=Horizontal, V=Vertical, D=Double   N

F = Letter Size:
  v =very small, s=small, e=elite, p=pica, l=large   P
  For enlarged letters: V,S,E,P,L

Printing Codes in Text   (# Symbolizes a Number)

`!tm#`	Top Margin
`!bm#`	Bottom Margin
`!lm#`	Left Margin - start text in #
`!rm#`	Right Margin - stop text in #
`!cj`	Center Justify
`!lj`	Left Justify
`!rj`	Right Justify
`!nh`	Normal line Height
`!sh`	Short line Height
`!sp#`	Spacing of text lines, 1 = single
`!pg#`	Next Page Number
`!hDX`	Make the Heading X
`!lp#`	Lines per Page
`!np`	Start a New Page
`!in#`	Indent or Outdent # Spaces
`!bs#`	Backspace # Spaces
`!nb`	Not Boldface
`!vb`	Boldface by Vertical repeat
`!hb`	Boldface by Horizontal repeat
`!db`	Bold face by Double repeat
`!sf`	Standard Font
`!if`	Italic Font
`!af`	Alternate Font

!us	Uniform character Spacing
!ps	Proportional Spacing
!ul	Underline
!nu	No Underline
!cm	Comment
!pcX	Transmit the Printer Code X

Normal Letters

!v1	Very Small
!s1	Small
!e1	Elite
!p1	Pica
!l1	Large

Enlarged Letters

!V1	Very Small
!S1	Small
!E1	Elite
!P1	Pica
!L1	Large
!ht	High Tiny superscripts
!lt	Low Tiny subscripts
!qt	Quit Tiny scripts

Print Specifications – Defaults

A	=	Left margin	7
B	=	Right margin	77
C	=	Top margin	2
D	=	Bottom margin	8
E	=	Spaces to Indent or Outdent (256 - X = Outdent X)	5
F	=	Spacing of Text Lines	1
G	=	Lines Per Page	66
H	=	First Page Number (0 = None)	1
I	=	Pause when new page? (Y/N)	N
J	=	Print if P, preview Slowly if S, preview Quickly if Q	S

INDEX

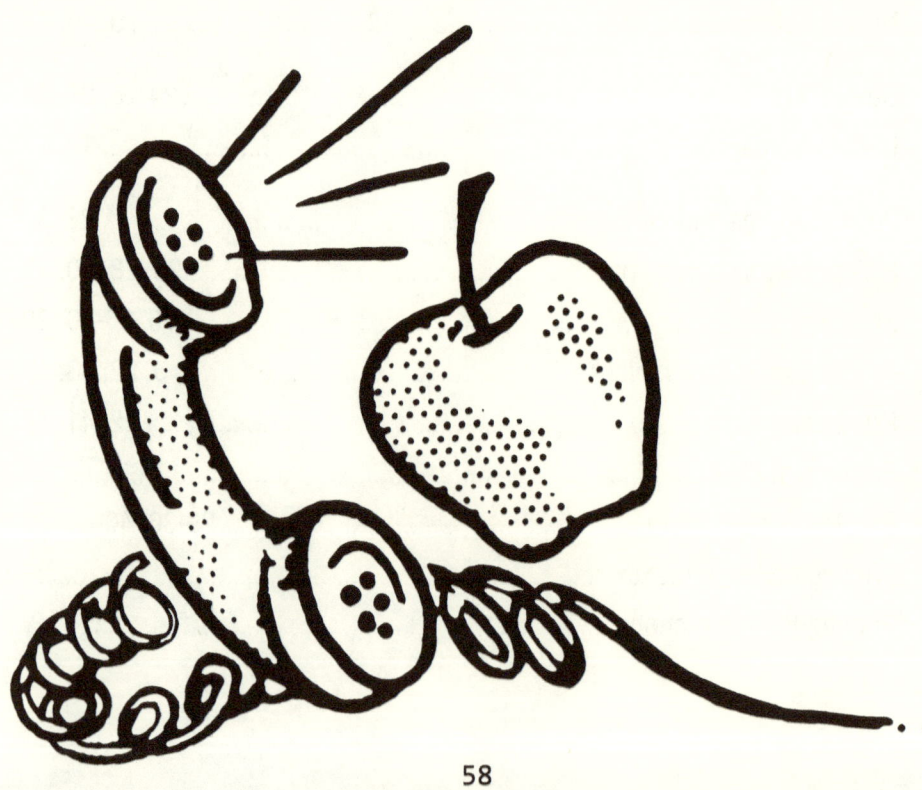